CURIOUS PEARL
SCIENCE GIRL

CURIOUS PEARL
MASTERS SOUND

An Augmented Reading Science Experience

by Eric Braun

illustrated by Anthony Lewis

PICTURE WINDOW BOOKS
a capstone imprint

CURIOUS PEARL

SCIENCE GIRL

Curious Pearl here!
Do you like science?
I sure do! I have all sorts of fun tools
to help me observe and investigate, but my
favorite tool is my science notebook. That's where
I write down questions and facts that help me
learn more about science. Would you like
to join me on my science adventures?
You're in for a special surprise!

This is a Capstone 4D book!

Want fun videos that go with this book?

Just visit www.capstone4d.com

Use this password

pearl.sound

I was getting ready to practice my recorder when there was a knock on the door. A voice called out, "It's me, Sal!"

Music to my ears! Sal is my good pal. I ran to open the door.

"Hey Sal, how are you?" I asked.

"Not good," he said. "My rabbit is sick. Without him, I can't do my magic show at the talent contest tonight. The prize is a summer pool pass!"

"Maybe I can help you win the prize," I said. "Let's have a snack and think of a plan."

After we got our snack, I played a few notes on the recorder. Sometimes music helps me think. But it was Sal who got the bright idea.

"Let's make a band!" he said. "You play the recorder, and I'll play the . . ."

Sal looked around for something to play. He grabbed a couple of pot lids and banged them together.

I noticed something. "Eureka!" I said.

"Eureka?" Sal said. "I thought you only said that when you make a discovery."

"Indeed, my pal Sal," I said. "Look how the music makes those crumbs vibrate."

"I don't get it," Sal said.

"Those jumping crumbs reminded me of something I read in one of my science books. Sound is made of vibrations." I pulled out my science notebook to write this down.

Sound is made when an object vibrates. The vibrations bump into the air and make it vibrate in waves. The sound waves travel through the air to our ears.

"Can we make our own instrument?" asked Sal.

"If we can make something vibrate, we should be able to make sound," I told him.

I found a paper towel tube and some wax paper. I wrapped the wax paper around the end of the tube and attached it with a rubber band. I poked a hole along the side of the tube.

Sal put the tube to his mouth and hummed. It made the wax paper vibrate, and that made music.

"Cool!" Sal said. He could cover and uncover the hole to change the sound, and he could hum higher and lower notes.

We played our instruments together. They sounded good, but something was missing.

"Let's call Sabina," Sal suggested. He called her and invited her to be in our band.

"That sounds awesome," Sabina said. "Be right over!"

After he got off the phone, Sal looked at me funny. I could tell he had a question on his mind.

"Pearl, I'm curious," he said.

Actually, *I'm* curious—Curious Pearl, that is— but I didn't interrupt him.

He said, "I get how sound is made of vibrations. But how does it travel through the phone? I don't notice the phone vibrating when I talk on it."

"Hmmm," I said. "Well I know the vibrations move through the air. But I don't know how it travels from one phone to another. Let's look it up!"

We found a website that explained how sound travels over distances with devices like telephones. I made a note in my science notebook.

A phone turns our sounds into an electrical signal. The signal travels through wires or the air and is converted back into sound by the other person's phone.

"Hey, guys!" my little brother, Peter, said. "Can I be in your band? I'm a good singer. Watch."

"You mean listen?" I said.

"That's what I said. Ready?" Peter sang a few lines about how he loves dessert. He is not a good singer.

"Maybe you should take a break," I said. "All that vibrating must be making you tired."

"I'm not vi-bating," Peter said.

"Vi-brating," I corrected. "And yes you were. Put your fingers on your throat when you sing. What do you feel?"

We all touched Peter's throat while he sang, "Cake and pie, cookies too, I love dessert, how about you?"

"Wow," Sal said. "You can feel his vocal cords vibrating in his throat."

"Cool," said Peter.

"Hey Peter, we don't need a singer," I said. "Would you like to play the rubber band-ophone?"

"The rubber what? I've never heard of that."

"That's because I just made it up," I said. "But I think it will rock."

We got a couple square containers from the kitchen and wrapped rubber bands around them.

"Pluck the bands," I said.

Peter plucked the band on the smaller container, and it went **bowwwww**. He did it again. "Cool," he said. Then he tried the bigger container. It went **boyyyyyy**. "It sounds different!"

"The rubber band on the bigger container is tighter," I said. "When you pluck it, it vibrates faster. That makes the air vibrate faster. And that makes a—different kind of sound."

"It's a higher sound," Dad said, walking through the room. "A looser band vibrates slower, and it makes a lower sound."

"I get it!" I said. I made a note in my trusty science notebook.

A sound's pitch is how high or low it is. There are even some sounds that animals can hear, but humans can't! Sound that is too high-pitched for us to hear is called ultrasound. Sound too low-pitched for humans to hear is called infrasound.

There was a knock on the door. "That's Sabina!"
Sal said.

"I'm here to make music!" Sabina said.

I grabbed two wooden spoons from the drawer
and a metal bowl. Then I found an empty yogurt
tub. "You can use these for drums," I said.

When Sabina hit the yogurt tub, it made a short wump sound because it vibrates for a short time. But when she hit the edge of the metal bowl, it went **binggg**. That's because the bowl vibrates longer than the yogurt tub.

A moving object has energy. When it collides with another object, energy is transferred from one object to the other, causing a vibration. The sound waves from this collision keep going until they run out of energy.

Finally we had all the instruments ready to go.
It was time to practice.

"Three, two, one . . ." I said.

We played for a while, until Dad came in
holding his ears.

"Uh-oh, are we playing too loud?" I asked.

"Well, my ears are ringing," he said.

"Sorry, Dad," I said. "I guess the sound vibrations are vibrating in your ears."

"That's true," Dad said. Then he explained how our ears work. I grabbed my notebook to write down the details.

The outer ear catches sound vibrations. It funnels the waves to the eardrum and to tiny bones that strike a nerve. The nerve sends a message to the brain, and you hear sound.

Sabina, Sal, Peter, and I practiced for the next hour. Then we went to the community center for the big talent contest.

We watched the first few acts. They were pretty good!

Then the announcer grabbed the microphone and introduced us. "Next up we have the Sound Squad performing their song, 'Vibrations in the Air'!"

Sal whispered to me, "I bet microphones work sort of like telephones. The sound waves are converted to electricity and get carried through a wire to the speakers. Then the speakers turn it back into the original sound."

"Eureka!" I said.

Our song went really well. I didn't know if we would win or not, but I had a lot of fun learning about sound and making music.

Sal felt the same way. "Thanks for playing with me," he said. "Win or lose, this was a blast."

Make Your Own Kazoo

You can build a kazoo just like Sal's and use vibrations to make music.

Here's what you need:

- cardboard tube from paper towels or toilet paper
- 4- x 4-inch (10- x 10-cm) square of wax paper
- rubber band
- something to poke holes (like a pencil)

Steps:

1. Wrap the wax paper over one end of the tube and secure it with the rubber band.

2. Using the pencil, poke a small hole in the side of the tube.

3. Put the open end of the tube to your mouth and hum. Hold your finger over the hole to change the sound.

You can hum higher and lower notes to change the sound your kazoo makes. If you want, you can decorate the tube with crayons or markers.

GLOSSARY

collision—when two things crash together and exchange energy

energy—the property that must be transferred between objects in order to perform work; similar to power

infrasound—sound that is too low for humans to hear

pitch—how high or low a note is; pitch is caused by how rapidly something vibrates

recorder—a musical wind instrument

ultrasound—sound that is too high for humans to hear

vibrate—to shake rapidly

vocal cords—membranes in the throat that vibrate to make sound

READ MORE

Braun, Eric. *Simply Sound: Science Adventures with Jasper the Origami Bat.* Origami Science Adventures. North Mankato, Minn.: Picture Window Books, 2014.

Duke, Shirley. *Waves of Light and Sound.* Let's Explore Science. Vero Beach, Fla.: Rourke Educational Media, 2014.

Johnson, Robin. *The Science of Sound Waves.* Catch a Wave. New York: Crabtree Publishing Company, 2017.

Midthun, Joseph. *Sound.* Building Blocks of Science. Chicago: World Book, Inc., 2012.

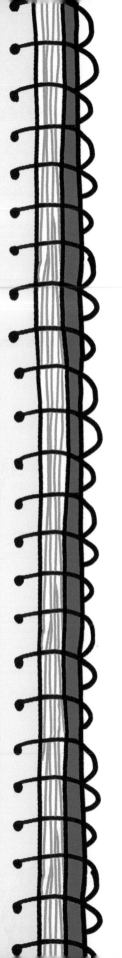

INTERNET SITES

Use FactHound to find Internet sites related to this book.

Visit *www.facthound.com*

Just type in 9781515829744 and go.

Super-cool stuff! Check out projects, games and lots more at **www.capstonekids.com**

CRITICAL THINKING QUESTIONS

How is sound made?

Some sounds are too high or low-pitched for people to hear. What is pitch? Hint: Use your glossary for help!

Pearl and her friends made instruments to make sound. Can you think of something you do that makes sound?

BOOKS IN THIS SERIES

INDEX

Thanks to our advisor for his expertise,
research, and advice:
Paul Ohmann, Ph.D.

Cover Illustrator: Stephanie Dehennin
Designer: Ted Williams
Art Director: Nathan Gassman
Production Specialist: Tori Abraham

The illustrations in the book were digitally
produced.

Picture Window Books are published by
Capstone, 1711 Roe Crest Dr., North Mankato,
Minnesota 56003
www.mycapstone.com

**Library of Congress Cataloging-in-
Publication Data**
Cataloging-in-Publication information is on file
with Library of Congress.
ISBN 978-1-5158-2974-4 (hardcover)
ISBN 978-1-5158-2983-6 (paperback)
ISBN 978-1-5158-2979-9 (eBook PDF)

Printed in the United States   5107